Drama and theatre as an avenue to resolve conflict between the Russians and Ukrainians.

By

Ocholi Augustine Egahi

DEDICATION

I dedicate my book to God almighty who has been my source of knowledge, wisdom and strength.

ACKNOWLEDGEMENT

My profound gratitude and appreciation goes to God Almighty who is my source of strength. May I use this medium to show gratitude to My parent Mr and Mrs Ocholi, my brothers and sisters Ocholi ojo Cecilia, Mrs Ochepo Ladi Ocholi, Ocholi Oloche Joseph, Ocholi Ochoechi Michael, Ocholi Benedicta Blessing and also my friends Sophia James, Ochoma Monday Bright, Monday Joseph Gyana, Umoru Damian,

Ahmed Peter Oloche and Gyana Suleiman Joseph for their advice and encouragement.

Introduction

You may be surprised to know that drama and theatre can play a role in resolving conflicts between different groups of people. For example, drama and theatre classes can offer a space for Russians and Ukrainians to explore their differences and find common ground. This is a valuable opportunity, as the media often portrays these two groups as being hostile towards each other. In this Work , I will explore how drama and theatre can help to resolve conflicts between Russians and Ukrainians.I WIll also look at some examples of successful theatre projects that have achieved this goal. Drama is one of the most vital aspect of arts. It gives more idea in to the inner motives of a writer and it also expresses the main essence of the writers work. Drama has played various function at different time and in different places. Conflict is seen in various parts of the universe as something odd but it can also be an agent of positive change in the society. There is an impulse in every human being that is demonstrated through drama, which is his oldest artistic experience that is used for entertainment and to educate people. As a discipline, drama has the capacity of sharpening social awareness and bringing alternative approaches to the problem of the society whether presented on stage or through the tube. Drama has abways been a means of communication that dramatist use in resolving conflict in the World and. This study brings valuable reasons that, drama and theatre are vital instrument for conflict resolution in World .

Table of contents

Drama and theatre for social Reform

Drama and theatre for reflection

Drama and Theatre for Mutual Understanding and Reconciliation

Theatre for therapy

Theatre for Participation

Drama and social problem

Drama as an instrument for conflict resolution in the world

What are the Benefits of drama and theatre?

Chapter one

Drama and theatre for social reform

In the historic period, drama's intention was once meant to play the leading position of carrying out religious rites and civic teachings. During this period, plays that have been carried out are meant to emphasize greater on instructing people in Other for them to be aware of how to go about their every day life's. As the years went by, dramatic pertormance that were executed have been intended to entertain human beings and this overall performance contained some content material of farces. In about the 18th century, dramatic performance have been done usually to inform the target market on social and moral problems in the society.

However, every target market has their personal reasons of going to the theatre to watch dramatical.performance. Some will say that, their intention is to seek knowledge, pleasure and some for curiosity. Drama is a literary form designed for public presentation and writing about drama explains how drama relates to the soCiety. Some scholars say that, drama is seen as a clear instrument for social change in the society while others say that, drama offers a skill for the Society to replicate upon itself and it's belief.

According to Richard Wilbur , drama is viewed as a tool for correction in the socicty. Richard Wilbur went in addition to say that, to tackle societal problems Is to expose it to the customary public and that can be performed only through dramatization (102). In every dramatic performance, there is always a performative factor and this component are found In each society.

These factors are considered in our celebralions, sport events and religious ceremonies (Brocket1991:1)".
Drama is drawn from every day experience and phenomenon in the

society, this phenomenon is viewed as conflict. Every society is bound to ride one form of conllict or the other. For instance, Nigeria being one of the greatest Country in AFrica which consists of different ethnic groups and exclusive non secular belief, has been worried with various types of conflicts right from it's origin.

This war may also either be ethnic, religious, cummunal, political and monetary conflicts. This conflict has left a permanent mark on the history of the nation. Such everlasting marks consists of the Aba and opobo women's insurrection in 1929, the coup in 1966, the Fulani's herdsmen and the Agatu people, the religious crisis in (Jos, Kaduna and kano), the sharia war in 1977, the oil war in 1986, the Tiv/Udam struggle in 2002 and most especially the Nigerian civil battle in 1967 Which have affected most Nigerians mentally. In spite of the etforts closer to resolving these conflicts, they still remain now not totally resolved. The proportion of the prevailing crisis are surely bringing out new weakness that appears to be threatening the Country today.

As a Matter of fact, Nigeria Been greater than any African country needs great efforts in fighting resolution. Drama in this regards is viewed as a quintessential and veritable instrument that can be used by way of dramatists to have interaction With human beings to participate actively in resolving fighting in Nigeria and in the world.

Theatre is frequently related with normal western stage overall performance for wealthy spectators with luxurious costumes and beautiful backdrops. While this is simply a very unique shape of theatre, there are moreover greater than a few other forms which have been used for features past mere entertainment, such as to deliver religious, educational, political, social or financial messages.

For instance, the use of theatre for the rationale of development has been an exercising in Northern Uganda considering that the mid-1980s. 'Theatre for Development' used to be at first stimulated by using ability of Paulo Freire, a Brazilian cultural and educational theorist and practitioner, who believed that people possess information with the aid of life time out but are persuaded with the resource of the oppressor to think about that their information is irrelevant. Stimulating human beings to come to be mindful and to generate records in their personal pursuits is referred to as the pedagogy of the oppressed (Freire, 1970).

This has influenced Freire's very own student, Augusto Boal, who developed the 'Theatre of the Oppressed': a structure of well-known theatre and for human beings designed to assist people study methods of resisting oppression in their day by day lives (Boal, 1982).

Initially, the use of theatre in a improvement surroundings has worried performing performs to supply sturdy social messages, with little or no target market participation. Gradually, the practicable of theatre as a platform of discussion and of exploring pertinent problems internal a unique local is being realized (Scott-Danter, 1999). There are normally three kinds of famous theatre: theatre produced with the aid of way of a theatrical crew however oriented towards the people; theater geared up by way of and for the people, with audience; and theatre prepared by using and for the human beings involving goal target market as section of the overall performance (Mdoe, 2002).

The first type entails actors, directors and dramatists producing for the neighborhood to inspire social change, by using the use of conveying schooling message and encouraging target audience to handle issues confronted via the use of their community. The second class of theatre is carried out with the aid of humans except expert understanding to modern-day testimonies containing factors from their neighborhood and human beings (ibid). The third category, moreover referred to as dialogue board theatre (Boal, 1982) or playback theatre, performs a nearby situation in the front of centered audience, and encourages them to intervene and be a section of in the act to unravel the situation, thereby formulating techniques to get to the bottom of their non-public problems.

Chapter two

Drama and theatre for reflection

Theatre as a media of verbal change constantly mirrors and shows the society. This has been emphasized via Yerima (2007), who quoted Shakespeare: "Theatre is a mirror for highlighting man's humanity and also a tool for grasp why man moreover finds it so undemanding to transgress that equal humanity". The dramatic illustration of real memories or phenomena brings the hidden values or questions in the society to people's awareness, as a outcome induces human beings to reflect on troubles (Aprill et al., 2006).

While we might also witness a special phenomenon and hear of someone's story in our day by day lives, they will now not have as strong an have an effect on without a dramatic illustration that engages people's emotions. Without art, authenticity doesn't mean much. According to Richard William (1970), the creator of the film Nil by using Mouth, which narrated the real life ride of alcoholism and drug-taking through way of a man recognized as Gary Oldman.

When actual existence experiences are captured inside the dramatic form, strong emotions and resonance can be aroused amongst target market and powerful consequences such as trade in attitudes, behaviours or even causes of lifestyles are practicable (Somers, 2008).

For this reason, famous theatre has been utilized to mission fact or a specific close by bother to records individuals and centered target target market into analyzing their private real-life stipulations (Mdoe, 2002). For instance, after the civil warfare in Mozambique between 1975 and 1992, a social survey and a theatre presentation have been performed amongst the displaced humans who remained in the vicinity of Nawagene (Scott-Danter, 1999).

While the social survey raised the problems of lack of local services such as want for clean water and handy health centres, the theatre presentation added out extra refined issues of social-relationship and the social motives inhibiting improvement (ibid). Theatre as a consequence sensitizes a neighborhood on priority issues. Apart from that, a Theatre for development

(TFD) exercise which was equipped by means of University of Abuja Nigeria theatre arts branch and attended by ocholi Augustine Egahi in 2017 at Gaba village in Bwari local authorities location in Abuja.

During the workout ocholi Augustine Egahi and his crew have been able to make lookup and sametime conscientizing the villagers about problems in the community and making them to be significantly aware of the state of affairs and issues of their neighborhood and making them see reasons why they profer options to the problem. This exercise used to be able to expand the fundamental consciousness of the Gaba villagers in order for them to replicate greater on their troubles that there had been no longer aware of in the society.

This is very tons so because, drama and theatre is an important hallmarks of literary project that reflects on the society and sametime can be used to profer lasting options for resolving conflicts.

For instance, the Russian and the Ukrainian battle that has being going on, a unique drama on display wishes to be carried out by way of quite a number talented and professional actors and actress of various nations in the world so as to tackle the issue of struggle as the theme and bringing resolution between two countries in the movie so as to increase the crucial consciousness of the Russians and the Ukrainians that drama which is considered as our ancient art structure has being enjoying a number roles even in the past and these days will serve as a veritable tool for conflict resolution in the world.

In so doing, this will allow every human being in the globe to be aware of the electricity of drama and how it can deliver unification of more than a few races of the world to come collectively and sametime profer options to combat that ravage the universe.

Chapter three

Drama and Theatre for Mutual Understanding and Reconciliation

Theatre can additionally function to bridge understanding among members in a community via offering an perception into others' factor of view (Kasoma, 1974). This occurs when tales are narrated from the point of view of a specific character, or when audience participate in acting different, or even opposite characters from themselves. For example, in the movie "Reaching Rural Families", a household planning employee performs the position of an ignorant mother, while the mom takes on the position of the household planning worker (ibid).

This promotes mutual understanding and reconciliation by way of allowing the target audience or actors to journey a different standpoint or a role. Someone who used to be earlier viewed as the different turns into familiar and beneficial properties empathy. The community receives a richer appreciation and extra complicated view of its personal people. Any motion towards social change might emerge from such adjustments in perception of self and others.

In Lebanon, forum theatre was once integrated into a struggle transformation framework in order to construct relationships between previously conflicting events by means of employing its capacity to relate, trip and recognize via bodily interactions, with and besides phrases (Reich, 2012).

On the other hand, when carried out for outsiders, theatre can sensitizes the authority or practitioners to the wants and aspirations of a community, and exhibit others their troubles to encourage more perception (Scott-Danter, 1999). One example is in Arua, Uganda, where a powerful piece of theatre on the theme of family overlook has been developed by using the local community.

The play captured, thru the stories of individuals of a family, a vary of interconnected issues from prostitution and alcoholism to home violence, faculty drop-out, early marriage and petty crime. At the cease of the performance, the audience consists of government and NGO officials were invited to discuss the troubles raised and the role of their institutions to tackle the root causes of the problems.

Apart from that, using James Ene Henshaw's This is our chance Which honestly suggests how drama and theatre brought mutual understanding between prince Ndamu of Udura and princess Kudaro of Koloro. This play truely brought mutual understanding between the long crisis between Koloro and Udura and additionally added reconciliation.

Chapter Four

Theatre for Therapy

A correct theatre may possess therapeutic effect, for each its participants and audiences. By watching or taking part in a play that is tightly connected to one's memory/personal story, one can re-categorize their memories, reedit their personal stories, and re-establish meanings from a complex, reflexive relationship between dramatic ride and non-public identity (Somers, 2008).

People find telling their tales fairly therapeutic, as pronounced by Scott-Danter (1990) about an ex-detainee who helped in a play about asylum seekers which took place in Oxford in 1997.

The Crude Theatre in Kibingo Village, Uganda for instance, invited ancient humans besides families to retell memorable events of their lives, serving as a therapy for the ancient and linkages across generations. For a specific crew of target audience who have faulty well-being however embarrassed to share the problems they are going through with these they experience may additionally now not understand, looking at a story which acknowledges and is aware thatissues and circumstances is itself enough to alleviate pain and fight isolation (ibid).

Theatre can illustrate a shared ride of many inside the equal neighborhood and affords de-solating effect, making humans recognise that they are no longer on their own in their struggles, and that they are somehow being understood through others.

Written with the aid of Somers, 'The Living at Hurford' dealt with the conflict of small family farms to stay in commercial enterprise following the foot and mouth sickness outbreak in

2001. A farmer approached after the performance and stated to Somers, 'That is my existence you put up there tonight.'

As a group which frequently finds expression of feelings difficult, farmers were in a position to furnish advice to the main character, Chaplain and shared his pain, for this reason imparting some varieties of restorations. These recuperation outcomes in the direction of each of the target audience and the actors themselves are vital for empowerment, meaning-making, identity formation and even collective awareness of social injustice, which can doubtlessly furnish seeds for future social transformation.

This is extra so because, theatre which is therapeutic in nature in the course of dramatic performance, permits the target audience to be engrossed in the dramatical moves making them feel more like it is taking place to them physically and most instances situations in dramatic performance that entails emotional moments about demise makes the target audience feels engrossed and most of them starts offevolved shading tears as though it is occurring to them in actual life.

Most especially, the actors and actress of such dramatic overall performance employs the use of "Realism and Naturalism " in the course of theatrical presentation so as to make it therapeutic to have an effect on the existence of the target audience positively.

For example, a dramatical overall performance on display about fighting between two countries where there may be bloodbath of so many lives can be presented through the use of Realism making the target audience sense engrossed and getting them conscious of the destruction that war brings to the world. This overall performance will expand the crucial consciousness of the audience and they shall comprehend the bad consequences of hostilities and they will no longer desire to be concerned in war.

Such form of movie performance needs to be introduced so that the Russians and the Ukrainians will understand that theatre and drama are powerful gadgets which are therapeutic in nature, which will get them aware that war only destroys lives and property and that theatre and drama is the only tool which can convey forth warfare resolutions to the battle ravaging them. In so doing, drama and theatre will be viewed as a sturdy avenue for resolving conflicts and people will be aware of the strength of arts via the media.

Chapter Five

Theatre for Participation

Theatre additionally serves as a participatory tool via inviting audience to take part in the act, making it an authentic two-way medium for speaking information. Forum theatre or playback theatre, for instance, transforms the target audience into actors and creators of the drama. Members of the audience are prompted to actively engage themselves in the process, severely reflect on venture and exchange the path of the play and strive out extraordinary solutions.

They can interrupt a performance and advise one-of-a-kind moves for the actors who in turn carried out their suggestions, as a result giving the spectators themselves a chance to come up with one of a kind solutions of a collective problem.

Theatre has been employed as a lookup tool by multiple development initiatives for engaging the neighborhood in a dialogue, and mobilizing communities to rally and help development activities.

One instance is the Primary Health Care (PHC) gadget in Malawi, which works together with the Chancellor College Theatre for Development group to probe, stimulate and tease out thoughts from the neighborhood (Kalipeni and Kamlongera, 1996).

The theatre team used a technique called "opening up the play", which includes asking direct questions to the target audience at vital points of the story line in the play and then incorporating their responses to the plot. As a result, a larger photograph of the community's fitness fame emerged. Everybody in the community contributed to the speak . The "play" nature of drama serves as a democratizing tool, as each person present at performances felt free to voice out their opinions.

Participation and self-expression, especially from those who regularly go unheard is stimulated. Apart from that, in 2017 when i was once in my year two we had been doing a production at the University of Abuja open Air Theatre. We had been producing a play titled Iredi war written through a Nigerian author Sam Ukala. During the path of the production, the members of the audience (M. O. A) was used to request questions and also added tips throughout the production. This tries to give an explanation to us how theatre is participatory in nature and brings harmony between communities, race and quite a number numerous nations to come collectively to carry forth understanding and discovering out troubles and sametime sorting out ways to profer solutions to those problems.

This is very a whole lot so because, a easy instance can additionally be viewed at some stage in any theatre for development workouts which it fundamental goal is to make bigger the integral consciousness of the neighborhood and get them aware of their issues through participatory theatres. In essence, theatre for participation can additionally be used as a capability of unifying various races and countries and sorting out issues and proffering options to those problems and i honestly consider that it can also be utilized to foster peace and unity between the Russians and the Ukrainians due to the fact that drama and theatre has verified how veritable there are in resolving conflicts and bringing peace to the world. In addition to this, this was the reason why i formed the "EGAHITARIANISM Theory" mainly to enable various races to come together as one and be unified. This is more so because, there's no need for disparity in the world but oneness to foster unification.

Chapter six

Drama and social problem

It is important to note that, social problems are as old as human society. According to Anele who explains that, societies often provide goals which individuals aspires to achieve for themselves.

In the process of achieving this personal goals and are gotten through the socially approved means, it is believed that they will be orderliness in the society but when it is not done in the socially approved way, it will bring disorderliness in the society. One of the earliest definition of social problems was made by Case (1924) in an article captioned "what is a social problem"?.

He defines social problems as a situation impressing a large number of competent observes as needing remedy by collective actions (Lemert 1980:29).

Also, social problem can also be seen as an issue that influence a considerable number of individuals within a society. Social problems started through social disorder and it is obvious that the recent social problems between the Russians and the Ukrainians started at the end of 2021 and was severe in 2022.

This issues in the society leads to social frustration and unhappiness, thus bringing about social problems. Here in the World, our society is marked by racism and religious differences. This days, in many places and at various stages, several things done are based on race and religious considerations.

For instance, the Russians felt that because there were the ones that colonized the Ukrainians so for that reason they kept threatening them towards minor issues thus bringing frustration among the Ukrainians regarded as inferior because they are their colonist.

This will therefore bring about social problems between the Russians and Ukrainians of which it has started already .

In every society, there is no social problem without a conflict thus when the social problem in the society becomes so extreme, it will therefore increase the conflict in the society. This actually made various theorist to express their view on the conflict theory. The theorist that stressed more on conflict theory is Karl Marx.

His theory is one of the theories that explains social phenomena. This theory places much emphasis on the conflict nature of social reality since it stresses social order rather than disorder and instability, which are social facts. Apart from Marx, other theorists like George Simmel's and Lewis Coser also wrote about the conflict theory.

Karl Marx.

Karl Marxs theory is found in German philosophy, English political economy, and French Socialism. Anele expresses Marx concept which stresses that, the extent to which man's knowledae is a reflection of nature as the same extent that his social knowledge is a reflection of the economic system of that society.

This assumption was developed based on Hegel's analogy of human philosophy. In a nutshell, Marx believed that human beings are prone to conflict over such scarce resources like wealth, Status and power. In the process of sourcing for this resources, it will bring about conflict and for Karl Marx, Conflict brings social change in the society.

George Simmel.

George Simmel's theory is often called "conflict functionalism". He explains that, unlike Karl Marx who says that conflict brings social change in the society, Simmel explains that the consequences of conflict functions towards social continuity.

Anele explains further that, George Simmel was concerned with the analysis of how conflict positively release consequences, which aid the maintenance of the entire society or soCial system. In essence, George Simmel was trying to say that conflict promote solidarity or unity in the social system or society.

Lewis Coser.

Lewis coser focuses his attention on the function of conflict. According to Coser he said that, despite the fact that conflict brings intense disagreement, it also serves as a form of socialization between individuals in the society or social system.

He went further and said that, conflict creates new norms for people in the society and it also leads to the formation of new association or groups.

Chapter seven

Drama as an instrument for conflict resolution in the world

Conflict is seen as a vital process to life that must be part of theatre. This statement explains the fact that without conflict theatre would not be able to create an experience of human existence.

Due to this, Debra Bruch said that, since the theatre can create a complete and living world centred on human being, conflict must be part of drama because life includes conflict.(Bruch, 1990:4). Some scholars said that, any play without a conflict is more like a monument.

In essence, when there is no conflict in drama, it is meaningless because the conflicts brings the actions in the drama. Also, Ngugi Wa ihiongo (1981) says that, drama and literature cannot escape from conflict because, it reflect directly and indirectly in our political, economic and social structures.

Suffice to say that, the afore mentioned assertion tries to sharpen our minds that drama and conflict are intertwined that they cannot do without each other so this clearly shows that the only remedy for resolving conflicts is through drama presentations by using the media as a tool of projector to the world how powerful drama is and i strongly believes that immediately this is done the war between the Russians and the Ukrainians will end in peace.

Due to these opinion by different scholars, Robert Cohen wrote about conflict in drama: Plot can hold suspense only when It involves alternatives and choices. Macbeth has strong reason to murder King Duncan and strong reasons not to, he had only the former or only the latter, he would project no real contlict and we should not consider him such an interesting character.

We are fascinated by a characters actions largely in light of the actions he rejects and the stresses he has to endure on making his decisions. In other words, plot entails not only the actions of a play but also the inactions... The things that are narrowly rejected and do not happen. A characters decision in list proceed from powerfully conflicting alternatives if we are to watch his behaviour with empathy instead of mere curiosity.

In watching a character act, the audience must also watch him think, a playwright gets him to think by pulling him Into conflict. Cohen's perception can also be seen in some of the plays written by important playwrights, who infuse conflict in their play's mainly to make the characters think and sort out ways or remedies of resolving the conflict. Despite the fact that conflict is a vital process to life that drama and theatre can not do without, drama is indeed a powerful and veritable means of resolving contlicts the world .

This is very much so because, it is a dynamic art form which functions as a means of entertainment, education ,celebration and at the sametime , serves as a powerful agent of social Change in the society. A clear illustration was actually made by

Hubert Ogunde in his play titled Yoruba Ronu (1964).

This play was dramatized to resolve the crisis between the Akintola's government and the western region in Nigeria.

The Akintola's government in the western region of Nigeria was too hostile with the people and he was having crisis with the people in the society so because of this Hubert Ogunde and his crew performed the

Yoruba Ronu (Yoruba think) in order for him to see and know that what his government was doing was wrong.

This play actually brought resolution between Akintola and the western region of Nigeria and it stood out as an eye opener for everyone to see the power of drama in resolving conflicts. Hubert Ogunde's view made many prominent Nigerian writers like Woke Soyinka, J.P Clark, Ola Rotimi , Ahmed Yerima and a lot of others to start writing plays and dramatizing on how drama can be used as a tool for conflict resolution not just in Nigeria but to the world as a whole.

Chapter eight

What Are the Benefits of Drama and Theatre?

You might be wondering, what are the benefits of drama and theatre when it comes to resolving conflicts between Russians and Ukrainians? Well, for starters, drama and theatre can provide a space for people to share their stories and experiences. It can also be a way for people to learn about each other's cultures and understand each other's point of view.

Most importantly, drama and theatre can help create dialog and build relationships between people who might not otherwise have a chance to talk to each other. And that's really the goal here: to find a way to resolve the conflict and move forward together. There are so many benefits of drama and theatre but i will discuss few relevant benefits and this includes :

i Empathy

ii Corporations and collaboration

iii Communication

iv Problem solving

Empathy

This is an important benefit of drama and theatre because it is seen as the capacity to understand another persons point of view in life. Acting roles from different situations, time periods, and cultures promotes compassion and tolerance for others' feelings and viewpoints. This is very much true because, drama and theatre are veritable tool which brings togetherness by making us understand various diverse cultures or countries in the world, to understand their perception towards life and sametime to tolerate each others in life.

Cooperation and Collaboration

Theatre combines the creative ideas and abilities of its participants. This cooperative process includes discussing, negotiating, rehearsing, and performing. This is afore mentioned statement is in alliance with what i said initially that it is important for various races in the world to perform a dramatic performance and and be projected via the media so that people can actually see the actual essence of drama and theatre. In do doing, it will enable various races to corporate, collaborate, negotiate and understand everyone's and perform this movie on drama as a tool for conflict resolution and both the Russians and Ukrainians will have a clear grasp of the Power of drama and theatre. In the process of this, empathy will be achieved between the Russians and Ukrainians and not only them other territories in the world.

Communication Skills

Drama enhances verbal and nonverbal expression of ideas. This is very much true because drama and theatre performance has always been used to communicate to the audience or the society. Theatre has a relationship with the society and that through drama and theatre communication can reach the society so that there will be fully equipped with vital information about problems and Means of solving those problems. For instance, the Russians and Ukrainians war which has caused the loss of lives and property between both nations, it's only through dramatization that both countries can be fully conscientize about what there are doing and that they should see the need for resolving the problem because no matter the vexation between both countries there's need for peace and orderliness between them and this can only be possible through drama and theatre.

Problem Solving

This is a vital benefit of drama and theatre in the society. Even in ancient and recent time, drama and theatre has been able to solve so many problems in the world. For example, In 2017 in Nigeria where the country is facing the problem of recession. This problem of recession was so severe that so many citizens were not able to afford food and making a living because there was inflation in the country's economy affecting the general price of every product in the country.

Due to this, artist came together to perform stage performance in every universities in Nigeria with the theme titled "Love and Recession". This particular stage play was actually stream live as the actions was going on in order for the government to look into this issue and find solutions to this issue. Immediately this was done, active solutions was made by the government and people went back to their normal life of purchasing things on the normal price.

In a nutshell, i'm trying to use this personal experience of mine to tell the world today how powerful drama and theatre is to resolve problem in the society and that it was actualize via the media.

Author's Note

We stay in a media culture, with battles of ideas and values. While artists and everyday humans might lack the political and monetary energy to implement changes, they possessed the ability to have an effect on feelings and thoughts via their work of acting and performing, which has probably greater profound influence on people's attitudes and mentality. Drama and Theatre are one such media that place artists and ordinary humans with tales that can become indirect activists, and make a contribution to their part toward achieving a higher world. Its promotion of reflection, reconciliation, therapy, participation and creativeness leads to empowerment of its contributors and spectators, turning them into manageable creators or resolvers of their personal circumstances. Drama and Theatre illustration of the modern environmental issues additionally add to its new necessary role of communicating scientific information. History affords proof for the workable of drama and theatre in producing lasting social impacts. Drama Theatre as a device thus deserves splendid recognition, research, support and advocacy from activists, academicians and donors as a valid approach to instill societal transformation.

Reference

Ocholi Augustine Egahi, A critical view of the African dream. 2022

Akashoro, G, Kayode, J. & Husseini, S. (2010). Theatre and Development: Opportunities and Challenges in a Developing World. In Communication 1(2): 107-112

Boal, A. (1982). The Theatre of the Oppressed (2nd Ed.). New York, USA: Routledge Press.

Bottoms, S. (2012). Climate Change 'Science' on the London Stage. WIREs Climate Change 3:339–348. doi: 10.1002/wcc.173

Carter, C. (2009). Artists and Social Change, Marquette, Michigan: Marquette University e-Publication. Retrieved from http://epublications.marquette.edu/cgi

/viewcontent.cgi?article=1026&context =phil_fac

Chaudhuri, U. (1994). There Must Be A Lot of Fish in that Lake': Toward an Ecological Theater."Theater 25.1: 23-31.

Clayton, S. & Opotow, S. (2003). Identity and Natural Environment: The Psychological Significance of Nature. Cambridge: MIT Press.

Curtis, D. (2003, Dec). Initial Impressions on the Role of the Performing and Visual Arts in

Influencing Environmental Behaviour. Paper presented at the TASA (The Australian Sociological Association) 2003 conference, University of New England, New South Whales, Australia. Retrieved from http://www.tasa.org.au/docs/conferences/2003/Environment/101103%20Curtis%20D.pdf

Curtis, D., Reeve, I. & Reid, N. (2007). Creating Inspiration: Using the Visual and Performing Arts to Promote Environmental Sustainability. Barton,

Australia: Rural Industries Research and Development Corporation. Retrieved from https://rirdc.infoservices.com.au/downloads/07-186

Etherton, M. & Ogubinyi, Y. (1988). Sub-saharan Arica:Popular, Political and People's Theatre. Communication Research Trends 9: 11-16

Felnor, M. & Orenstein, C. (2006). The World of Theatre: Tradition and Innovation (Sample Chapter). New Jersey, USA: Pearson. Retrieved from http://www.ablongman.com/samplechapter/0205360637.pdf

Freire, P. (2007). Pedagogy of the Oppressed. New York, USA: Continuum.

Heinlein, K. G. (2006). Green Theatre: Proto-environmental Drama and the Performance of Ecological Values In Contemporary Western Theatre. PhD. Dessertation. Louisiana State University and Agricultural and Mechanical College, Los Angeles, USA. Retrieved from http://etd.lsu.edu/docs/available/etd-1

1162006-175114/unrestricted/Heinlein_dis.pdf

Ho, P. (2012). Out of the Box: Positive Development and Social Change through the Arts. In Danah Boyd, John Palfrey and Dena Sacco (Eds.), The Kinder and Braver World Project: Research Series. Born This Way Foundation & Berkman Centre for Internet & Society at Harvard University.

Hosking, B & Penny, C. Playback Theatre as Methodology. Retrieved from http://www.playbacktheatre.org/resources/articles-and-books/

Kalipeni, E. & Kamlongera, C. (1996). The Role of "Theatre for Development" in Mobilising Rural Communities for Primary Health Care: The Case of Liwonde PHC Unit in Southern Malawi. Journal of Social Development in Africa 11(1):53-78

Kamlongera, C. (1996). Chapter 28: Theatre and Development in Africa, in Oscar Hemer & Thomas Tufte (eds.),

Media & Glocal Change: Rethinking Communication for Development (pp. 435-452)

Kasoma, K. (1974, May). Theatre and Development. Paper presented at an International Workshop on "Communication for Social Development" held at the University of Zambia, Lusaka.

Kidd, R. (1981). Domestication Theatre and Conscientization Drama in India. In R.Kidd & N. Coletta (Eds.) Traditions for Development: Indigenous Structures and Folk Media in Non-formal Education. Berlin, Germany: German Foundation for International Development and International Council for Adult Education.

Korza, P & Bacon, B. S. (2010). Trend or Tipping Point: Arts & Social Change Grantmaking - A 2010 Report for Funders. Washington, DC: Animating Democracy.

Malik, M., Raha, K., & Kidd, R. (1988). India: People's Theatre in A Perfomative Culture of 3000 Years.

Communication Research Trends 9: 5-10.

McKibben, B. (2005, Apr). "Imagine That: What the Warming World Needs Now is Art Sweet Art." Grist Organization. Retrieved from http://grist.org/article/mckibben-imagine/

Mdoe, A. R. (2002, Aug). Popular theatre and Its role in Participation for Social Development. Paper presented at the Dialogue for Change: Popularizing Policy and Influencing Change through

Action Research, Advocacy and Creative Communication in Livingstone Club Hotel, Tanzania.

Munk, E. (1994) "A Beginning and End." Theater 25.1: 5-6.

Reich, H. (2012). The Art of Seeing: Investigating and Transforming Conflicts with Interactive Theatre. Berlin: Berghof Foundation /Online Berghof Handbook for Conflict Transformation. Retrieved from http://www.berghof-handbook.net/doc

uments/publications/reich_handbook.pdf

Rizoaica, F. Learning from Forum Theatre Experiences – Acting Out the Solutions. Presentation slides retrieved from ec.europa.eu/education/grundtvig/doc/conf10/w9/forum.pdf

Rosenblatt, R. (2000, Apr/May). "Earth Day 2000: All the Days of the Earth." Time. Retrieved from http://eolit.hrw.com/hlla/rw/index2.jsp?Chapter=62&Page=1

Schechner, R., Boal, A. & Turner, V. (1988). A Theatre One Step From Life. Communication Research Trends 9: 1-4

Scott-Danter, H. (1999). Theatre for development: a dynamic tool for change. In Forced Migration: pp. 22-24

Smith, A. (2007). Raising Environmental Awareness through Performing Arts. Master Thesis. The Evergreen State College, Washington, USA. Retrieved from http://archives.evergreen.edu/masterst

heses/Accession86-10MES/Smith_A%20MESThesis%202007.pdf

Smith, J. (2011). Why climate change is different: six elements that are shaping the new cultural politics. In R. Butler, J. Smith & R. Tyszczuk (Eds.) Culture and Climate Change:Recordings. Cambridge, UK: Shed.

TINFO (Theatre Info Finland). (2012). TINFO News –Theatre and Ecology. Kerava, Finland: Author. Retrieved from http://www.tinfo.fi/dokumentit/tinfo_

news_2012_theatre_and_ecology_web_3105121111.pdf

UNESCO & CCVIS (2006). Act, Learn and Teach: Theatre, HIV and AIDS Toolkits for Youth in Africa. Paris, France: UNESCO.

United Nations. (1992, June). Agenda 21. United Nations Conference on Environment & Development in Rio de Janerio, Brazil.

Wasserman, S. & Young, M.F. (2013). The Great Immensity: A Theatrical

Approach to Climate Change. The Museum Journal 56(1): 79-86

Williams, R., The Guardian Review, 10.10.97, p. 6Yerima, A. (2007). Theatre, Culture and Politics. Lagos: Concept Publication Limited.

Anele. A. K. Social change and social problems Owerri: Springficld publishers 1 Anele, A. K.. Socia/

Arendt, H. On Violence, New York: Harcourt Brace and World. (1969), pringficld publishers 1999

Barclays. A matter of honour. Port Harcourt: Dec Gold-linger Publishers 1999 Ayakoroma, Barclay Publishers 1999

Bachrach, P. and Baratz, M. S. The two faces of power' in Scott, John (ed.), Power, Volume 2 Bachrach, P. and Bar

Bamidele, L. O. Literature and sociology Ibadan :Stiring-lorden publishers Nigeria Ltd, 2000

Bantock.A. An introduction to sociology. New York Basic Books, Inc, 1975.

Beetham, D. The Legitimation of Power, Houndmills: Macmillan.

Brockett. G. Oscar. Fistory of the Theatre. Sixth edition. Needham Heights: A Division of Simon and Schuster Inc, 1991.

Brunch Debra. Conflict Glencoe. The free Press, 1990.

Castells, M., The Rise of the Network Society, Volume I of the Information

Age: Economy Society and Culture, Oxford:Blackwell Publishers. (1991).

Dahi, R. A. A critique of the ruling elite model. in Scott, John (ed.), The Sociology of Elites, Volume1, Aldershot: Edward Elgar Publishing. (1958).

anl, R. A. Further reflections on "the elitist theory of democracy, American Political Science Review 60: 296 305. (1966).

Dahl, R. A. Who Governs? New Haven: Yale University Press. (1971)

ABOUT THE AUTHOR

Ocholi Augustine Egahi is a Nigerian writer born on sixth March 1995 from Benue State located in the northcentral section of Nigeria. He is the last in his household and he grew up in the Army Barracks because his Father is a military personnel in the Nigerian Arm force. He had his elementary school in L. E. A angwandodo gwagwalada Abuja (2000-2006). He then obtained admitted in to Bec international college where he bagged his west Africa examination council certificate in 2012. During this period, Ocholi Augustine Egahi performs and loves football and used to be acknowledged to be the pleasant in his pairs but due to the truth that his Dad desired him to study in the university he had to end football. He enrolled in to the University of Abuja Nigeria and was granted admission in the department of Theatre arts. After four Years in the

University he graduated with second class upper top division in bachelor's degree in arts. During his Years in the university, he joined the Theatre arts soccer crew and he used to be the exceptional player in the team and in the academic discipline was known to be very intelligent in his writing and was recognised to be a dramatic theorist due to his writing, innovative and talking prowess. After his graduation, he served his Nigeria for one year in the Nigerian national youth service corp where he additionally bagged the NYSC certificate. Immediately that, Ocholi Augustine Egahi commenced his writing capacity and was once honestly inspired by using most white writers like Lester Sumrall, Kathryn Kuhlman, Smith Wiggleworth, St. Patrick, John Eckhardt, Henrik Ibsen, Albert Camus, writers in realism, Elizabethan writers and third generation writers in Africa and writers who spoke on neo-classism and Negritude.